First US edition 2022

Library of Congress Catalog Card Number 2021953455
ISBN 978-1-5362-2850-2

22 23 24 25 26 27 CCP 10 9 8 7 6 5 4 3 2 1

Printed in Shenzhen, Guangdong, China

This book was typeset in AT Arta.
The illustrations were done in ink, watercolor, and acrylic paint.

Candlewick Press
99 Dover Street
Somerville, Massachusetts 02144

www.candlewick.com

For Donna and Joan
MJ

For Judith, Martin, Helen, David, and Annie
and our times spent by the sea
JD

CANDLEWICK PRESS

PUFFIN

illustrated by

MARTIN JENKINS   JENNI DESMOND

If you've ever visited the seaside, you've probably seen a lot of seabirds. Exactly which kinds (there are tons) depends on where you've been. Near me, I can usually spot guillemots and little auks zooming around, fulmars and gannets wheeling overhead, several kinds of noisy gulls, and sometimes even a fierce-looking skua.

2

But of all the different seabirds, there is one kind that is my absolute favorite. They're not the biggest or the quickest or the loudest. They've got bright orange feet and plump little bodies and the best bills ever (well, in spring and summer at least).

Can you guess what they are?

They're puffins!

To see puffins, though, you
have to be patient. They're not always
here. They spend the winter far out at sea.

4

Sometime early in spring, the first ones appear, bobbing around in the ocean near the shore. Every day there are a few more. Then, one evening, they all take off in a great flock. They circle around for a while as if they're wondering whether it's safe to land. Eventually one takes the plunge, then another, then another. At last—they're home!

The new arrivals have a careful look around and then set off to check out last year's burrow—they have a good memory for that sort of thing and know just where to find it. Often the first thing they'll meet is . . .

5

last year's mate.

They look as if they're pretty happy to see each other.
They clatter their bills together while slowly stomping
their feet, making quite a racket.

The next job is to inspect the burrow.

A puffin's bill becomes brightly colored in the spring; in winter it fades to mostly gray.

Sometimes, though, someone else is already there,
making themselves at home.

We can't
have that!

That's better.
Time for a look inside.
It'll probably need to be
cleaned up a bit.

Ack!

Or even
repaired . . .

A few sprigs of soft grass
and everything's ready.
And now what? It all gets
a lot quieter.

Each day one of the puffins disappears into their burrow while its mate flies off to sea.

The puffin stays in there for hours, popping out every now and then for a good look around (or a quick poop).

Eventually its mate returns.
The two puffins say hello to each other,
usually with a bit of bill-clattering,
then swap places.

And all this goes
on for days . . .

and days . . .

and days.

So what's going on
down there?
Let's take a peek!

One of them is sitting on an egg!

Puffins lay only one egg each year. The male and female take turns sitting on it.

Weeks and weeks go by.

Then, one day, a tiny hole
appears in the eggshell.
Slowly the hole grows
and grows . . .

until the whole shell
cracks open and . . .

out pops
a baby
puffin.

Now the hard work starts. The chick needs to be kept warm and dry,
and its parents have to feed it—puffin chicks have big appetites.

While one parent stays to look after the chick, the other one heads out to sea to fish, storing its catch neatly in its bill.

Puffins feed their young mainly on small fish, especially sand eels.

Once it's got enough,
it heads home.

Puffins normally store about ten fish in their bill at once— sometimes as many as a hundred!

Off flies the other parent to take its turn fishing.
Back and forth they go, day after day,
as the chick grows bigger and bigger.

Things are normally peaceful,
but every now and then . . .

Oof!

What on earth was that?

An Arctic skua after a free lunch.

They're always stealing fish from other birds.

Nothing to do but head back out and try again.

After six weeks, the chick has grown a lot. It often comes out of its burrow to look around and stretch its wings, always ready to dash back in if it spots a hungry gull or skua overhead. Its parents spend less time feeding it, too.

One night, when most skuas and gulls are off asleep somewhere, the chick carefully makes its way out of the burrow.

and then,
all at once,
it's gone.

After practicing a few
wing-flaps and a jump or
two, it's up in the air . . .

The young puffin is on its own now.

It has to learn how to dive and catch fish and survive the winter storms all by itself. It's hard, and not all young puffins survive. But with luck, in a few years, one spring it'll be bobbing around near the shore, looking for a mate and getting ready to find a nice warm nesting site of its own.

All About Puffins

There are three different kinds of puffins. Two of them, crested puffins and horned puffins, are found in the northern part of the Pacific Ocean. The third kind, called Atlantic puffins or often just puffins, is found in the northern part of the Atlantic Ocean. These are the puffins in this book.

Crested Puffin

Horned Puffin

Atlantic Puffin

In addition to having their food stolen by Arctic skuas, puffins are sometimes killed and eaten by great skuas and great black-backed gulls. Puffins that aren't eaten can live for more than forty years.

Each female puffin lays one very large egg a year. It takes from thirty-nine to forty-five days to hatch, and the chick will spend several days pecking its way out of the shell. When the young puffin (sometimes called a puffling) first leaves its nest, it doesn't look at all like its parents. It takes on its adult colors when it's four or five years old and ready to breed.

Atlantic puffins breed in big colonies, mostly on islands and at the tops of cliffs along the coastlines of Europe. Some also breed in the western part of the Atlantic, around Greenland, in Newfoundland, and as far south as Maine. No one knows exactly how many Atlantic puffins there are, but it's quite a lot, probably between 10 and 12 million. More than half breed in Iceland.

Index

Look up the pages to find out all about these puffin things. Remember to look for both kinds of words: this kind and this kind.

Find Out More

If you'd like to learn more about puffins, visit these websites:

Audubon Project Puffin: projectpuffin.audubon.org

Bird Spot: www.birdspot.co.uk/bird-identification/puffin

Cornell Lab of Ornithology: www.allaboutbirds.org/guide /Atlantic_Puffin/

National Geographic Kids: www.kids.nationalgeographic.com /animals/birds/facts/atlantic-puffin